101 Ways to Be a Special Dad

☆

101 Ways to Be a Special Dad

VICKI LANSKY

Illustrations by Kaye White

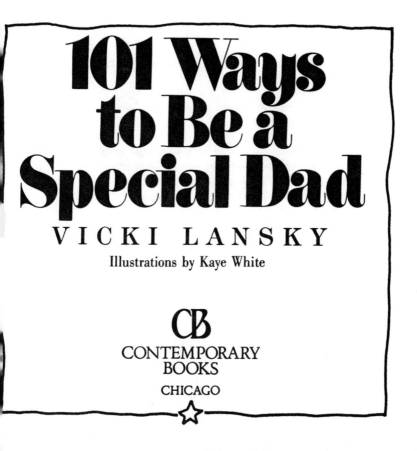

CB

CONTEMPORARY
BOOKS

CHICAGO

Library of Congress Cataloging-in-Publication Data

Lansky, Vicki.
    101 ways to be a special Dad / Vicki Lansky.
        p.   cm.
    ISBN 0-8092-3820-9
    1. Fatherhood—United States—Miscellanea.
  2. Father and child—United States—Miscellanea.
I. Title.   II. Title: One hundred one ways to be a special
Dad.   III. One hundred and one ways to be a special
Dad.
HQ756.L36   1993
306.874'2—dc20   92-41271
                                              CIP

Published by Contemporary Books, Inc.
Two Prudential Plaza, Chicago, Illinois 60601-6790
Manufactured in the United States of America
International Standard Book Number: 0-8092-3820-9

Special thanks to all the dads

who have shared with me over the years

who love to (and do) play with their children
with or without this book

who specifically shared their expertise with
me: Phil Courter, Randall Horton, Chris
Johnson, Bruce Lansky, James Levine, Peter
Lowry, Harvey Plotnick, and David Stewart

☆

Foreword

Any parent who doesn't know Vicki Lansky should. For almost two decades—ever since she wrote *Feed Me, I'm Yours* and *The Taming of the Candy Monster*—she's been offering practical advice for the well-intentioned and often overwhelmed of our species.

What's always made Vicki's work unique is its grounding in the real-life experiences of parents. She's constantly talking to parents, parents from Portland, Maine, to Portland, Oregon, parents from northern Minnesota to southern Alabama. More important, she's always listening. She's ever vigilant to hear the little things that work.

☆

In this book, for the first time, Vicki has put the spotlight on dads. But as usual, she's listened hard. From our work with thousands of fathers, I know that Vicki's tips—some familiarly confirming and others brand new—will help you stay connected to your kids.

James A. Levine
Director, The Fatherhood Project
Families and Work Institute
New York, New York

Introduction

Let's hear it for dads! They bring something very special to parenting that really is different from what moms bring. But sometimes fathers forget their special knack for parenting in the busy-ness of everyday life. I don't think there is a dad out there who wouldn't love a few more ideas to draw upon.

Well, here are 101 of them. They are easy to read and easy to do and will warm the hearts of kids and dads alike. How do I know? Because I've gathered them from other dads who enjoyed these activities or found these tips to be of value. So take a minute to get some new ideas—or remind yourself of old ones—and enrich your parenting repertoire. Most

☆

activities are written as one-on-one activities but can be adapted to include some or all of your children.

Speaking from a mom's point of view, I can add that I think 90 percent of good parenting is just being there. It's not always easy. If work keeps you from it, you might consider coming home for dinner and some family time, if distance allows, and then heading back to the office. You'll have to work later, but the time you spend with your kids means far more to them than you can imagine. If dinner is not realistic, encourage the kids to join you with their dessert for some conversation while you eat. At any rate, work to set aside some part of each day for spending time together. In today's world, quality

☆

time is not something easily come by. It's something you have to make time for.

Your kids can learn from you that dads cry, get scared, and make mistakes. Avoid saying things like "Big boys [girls] don't cry." They do. Learn to say, "I know you feel bad [hurt/are scared]. I love you. Let me hold you," and "Whoops, I goofed. I'm sorry." Tears are not a sign of weakness for adults or children. Tears are usually an outlet for pain—physical or emotional—that is better released than stored.

The best fathering tip is one you've probably heard before but is worth repeating: Love (or, at least, respect) your children's mother, and let your

☆

kids see that you do. Children remember all affectionate moments between parents—as well as every scary, angry fight. Choose your words and actions carefully. They are your children's true inheritance.

Vicki Lansky

101 Ways to Be a Special Dad

☆

Making up tales to tell your child is easy if you remember a few basic guidelines: Always start with "Once upon a time. . . .";
use your name, your child's, and fanciful ones (for example, Antonia Elonza Biminini) for recurring characters; don't be afraid to use a bit of suspense or violence; and, if stuck for an ending, let the story be resolved with magic (a little Presto! or Abracadabra!).

...and her name was Georgene, just like yours!

Bring your child to work with you during or after hours every now and then. Your child will love a tour of your workplace, a demonstration of your job, and an introduction to your boss and coworkers if appropriate. If you work in an office, set up a workstation with paper clips, staples, pencils, paper, calculator, and similar items to keep your little "temp" busy.

Turn a frown into a giggle with this trick: Pretend your other features are levers that control your tongue. Push on your nose with your finger and stick your tongue out; pull on an earlobe and swing your tongue to the opposite side; retract your tongue when you pull on your Adam's apple. You

can let your child do the pushing and pulling, and then see if his or her tongue moves when *you* push or pull!

Take your child on a wheelbarrow ride around the yard next time you are working outside. Clean wheelbarrows are probably more popular with Mom, but don't let a dirty one deter you. Your child will enjoy it even more!

Throw a ball or birdie
at any kind of racket held
by a child five or older.
He or she will love
simply connecting with
it. Teaching your child to
swing the racket will come later.

Have your child help you design and hang a sign that says "Gone fishing!" Take along a rod, reel, and fishing license for both of you (if needed) and some bait. Bait shop or sporting goods store personnel will be glad to tell a novice fisherman how to go about using the equipment and choosing suitable bait. If you don't like to use live bait, fish for something that doesn't require it.

☆

Take a child or two with you when you run an errand. Children can participate in many ways, such as dropping letters in the mailbox, selecting grocery items such as cucumbers or cereal, counting change, or carrying a purchase for you.

☆

The best place to play with a child of any age is probably on the floor or ground. Let an infant fall asleep on your chest, play gymnastics, share a board game, read to your child, or just look up at the ceiling or sky. Getting down will lift your spirits and enhance your quality time together.

☆

Rainy day? Build a hideout for your child. You can make a fortress out of blankets and couch cushions, or simply duck under the bed covers.

Crawl in,

. . . taking a flashlight and some
books to read or a game to play together.

Play Sock Ball.
Place a solid but not
hard ball at the bottom
of a tube sock and knot it.
Swinging and tossing it by
the "tail" makes tossing
easier for kids. It's also
easier to catch because
there is more of it!

Take your kids to a miniature golf course. They can each pick just the right-sized club for them and a ball in their favorite color. Don't give too much instruction, forget about making par, and just enjoy yourselves. After you all finish the game, celebrate with some refreshments and relive the best moments and worst shots.

Take a drive into the country to a pick-your-own orchard or farm. (Check your local classified ads for locations.) From strawberry season in June to the pumpkin harvest in the fall, there is a long harvest season—during which children can learn that food is only *sold* in stores, not *grown* there.

⭐

Planting a tree, bush, or houseplant? Make your child your official gardening assistant and work together. Continue to work together—watering, weeding, and watching it grow—and your growing thing will be permanent testimony to the time you spent together.

Doesn't every dad read the comics to his kids in bed on Sunday mornings? If you don't do this, you're missing out on one of fathering's greatest pleasures. (It's never too late to start!)

☆

Set aside an extra set of simple workshop tools and materials for your child to use while you are working with your own tools. Extra wire and wood, a screwdriver, and a hammer can be the basis for wonderful creations. You can admire each other's work! Teach your child the names of tools, so that he or she can assist you by handing you what you need.

☆

Do you like roller-coaster rides? If you enjoy going on fast rides at amusement parks, your child will like being introduced to them in the safety of your company.

There's nothing better than holding on to Dad when scared or excited.

Play soccer with your child.

It's a good game for young children because they can kick a ball more easily than they can throw one. You may find it easier and less competitive to practice dribbling around a tree or around each other rather than kicking the ball back and forth.

☆

Take a trip to a train station.

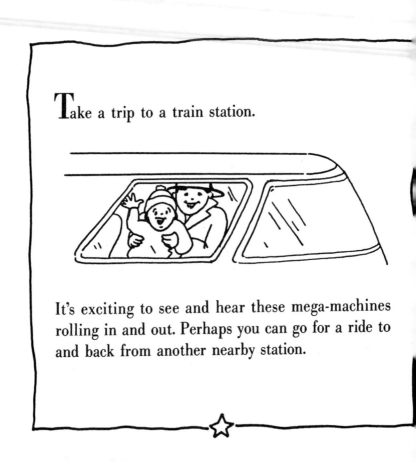

It's exciting to see and hear these mega-machines rolling in and out. Perhaps you can go for a ride to and back from another nearby station.

Team up
with your child
to cook!

On weekends you and your child can be responsible for at least one breakfast or lunch, whether you make pancakes, French toast, or grilled cheese sandwiches. Make it a family tradition.

If you don't have a loving nickname for your child, create one (nothing sarcastic). It can become a very special, personal form of endearment a child will remember fondly over the years.

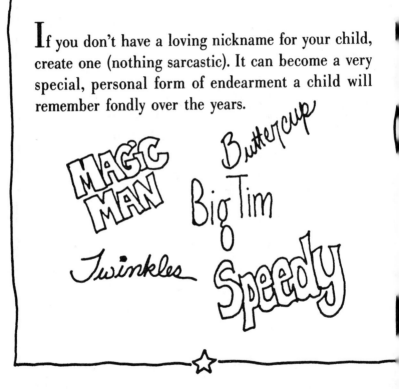

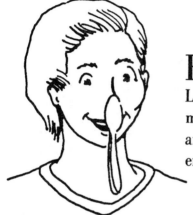

Razzle-dazzle 'em!
Learn one or two
magic tricks
and use them to
entertain or divert.

Try the simple "spoon-hanging-from-the-nose feat."
(Warm the spoon by breathing on it or rubbing it
with your fingers to make it adhere.) Then pretend
the spoon is stuck to your nose and has to be torn
off!

☆

The next time you're near a lake or pond, teach your child to skip stones.

Show him or her how to pick just the right kind of stones—smooth, round, and flat—and demonstrate the correct technique for skipping—with a low, skimming side throw. As your child becomes more skillful, see who can skip a stone the farthest or the most times.

☆

$$\begin{array}{r} \underline{1}\ \text{TOUCHDOWN} = 6 \\ 1\ \text{CONVERSION} = 1 \\ +\ 1\ \text{FIELD GOAL} = 3 \\ \hline 10 \end{array}$$

Are you a sports fan? Next time a big game is on TV, explain the objective and the basic rules to your child. Tell him or her what makes a good play. You might just create a sports buddy for yourself! Kids can even practice simple math skills by keeping track of the score.

Establish a bedtime routine that includes a special question for your child, such as:

"What is the best thing that happened to you all day?"

"Who did you thank/hug/help today?"

"What are you going to dream about tonight?"

Don't forget to include

"I love you"

in your good-night chat.

Next time you are working outdoors, give a very young child a clean, good-sized paintbrush, a bucket of water, and instructions to "paint" the house, fence, or sidewalk. As water temporarily darkens the surface, your child will have the feeling that he or she is actually painting.

☆

Let your child be your navigator on a drive around the neighborhood. A younger child can decide for you whether to turn right, turn left, or go straight at intersections on the way to the shopping center. An older child can handle a map marked with a highlighter pen to track a longer trip.

Every child—male or female—can learn (with Dad's help!) how to tie a tie. Begin with the tie around the neck with the thick end on the left. Adjust it so the thick end is twice as long as the thin end on the right. Wrap the thick end over the thin one, around and up over the neck V, and around, up, and down through the "tunnel." You should be looking in the mirror together while working on this. Give your child one of your old ties to keep and practice with.

Make library outings during your time together. Get in the habit of picking one book to read there and bringing the others home.

P.S. There's nothing wrong with enhancing your status with books that favor fathers, such as *A Perfect Father's Day* by Eve Bunting or *The Summer Night* by Charlotte Zolotow.

☆

Designate some or all of your loose pocket change as "kids' savings," to be divided each evening between your children. Have those who are old enough count it before it goes into a piggy bank. This practice may keep your dresser top less cluttered, and it will surely encourage your child in a savings habit.

Camp out with your child. If you're not a pro, start out by camping in your backyard and then move up to a local campsite. Gather your gear, including sleeping bags and flashlights. Set up the tent together and delegate as many of the tasks as you realistically can.

Turn on loud, fast music, tuck a small child under each arm, and spin around until you all collapse in a dizzy heap. It's silly and exhausting fun that never hurt anyone.

☆

Go fly a kite—together!

Choose a simple, easy-to-fly type and a day with a lot of wind. Bring repair supplies along with you. Make your child feel that he or she is in charge by letting him or her hold the string while you run the kite. Let your child do as much of the kite flying as possible.

Share with your child the story (any version will do) of the pot of gold at the end of a rainbow. Look for a rainbow together if the sun comes out after a rain shower. Or make your own rainbows:

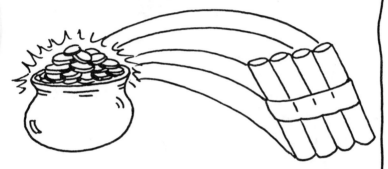

Tape together several crayons so you can draw rainbows on paper indoors or pieces of colored chalk to use on sidewalks and driveways outdoors.

☆

Question: Why is it that all dads give children rides on their shoulders?

Answer: It doesn't matter why, just don't stop doing it! Kids love a chance to be bigger than grown-ups, so this is always a treat for them.

If you're a "travelin' man," call home daily to speak to your son or daughter. Ask your child for details about the day's events. Afterward, ask to speak to his or her fabulous mother— a surefire heart-warmer for your child as well as your spouse.

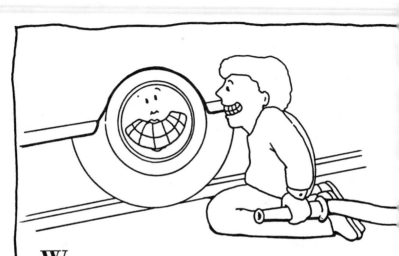

Wash your car with your child's help. Kids mix well with huge sponges, soapy water, and a hose. You'll enjoy each other's company, and who knows, if it turns into a water fight on a warm day, that can be a lot of fun, too. Afterward, go for a ride to show off your work.

Write poems and stories about your children to share with them at bedtime or another quiet time. There is no better way to tell people you love them than to create something unique for them.

I love my
little Emmy,
She's as sweet
as she can be.
One day she didn't
tie her shoe
then she tripped
and skinned
her knee!

Help your child
learn how to somersault!

Count how many
your child can do in a row.
Do them together. A child will delight in the
silliness of Dad doing a somersault.

icky

Picky
Quicky
sticky

Ask your child to think of rhymes for an easy base word, such as *icky* or *nose*. This is a fun way to pass time while driving or waiting in a restaurant.

☆

Did you collect coins when you were a kid? Explore that hobby again or for the first time with your child. Help him or her decide what type of coins to collect. Purchase a book to house your child's collection, visit coin stores, check out library books on the subject, and inspect pocket change for unusual pieces.

☆

You don't have to be an art lover to enjoy museums. Take your child to one of those "other" museums, such as children's, science, or natural history museums or a planetarium. Kids are always a good excuse to explore some of those places you've been meaning to get to yourself.

Drop off your child at day care or school on your way to work, or take the evening pick-up shift. It's not only a fair share of the responsibility, but it gives you special time alone with your child. Surprise your child one afternoon (let Mom in on the secret) when you pick him or her up and go on a picnic, to a movie, or out for dinner.

☆

Let your child dance with you to your favorite music—first as a baby in your arms, later as a child standing on your toes. As your child gets older, take turns picking selections to dance to. It's a wonderful way to be close to your child and keep up with current music trends at the same time.

Teach your child to make a finger face mask and become an official member of the Junior Birdman Club: Form a circle with each thumb and index finger. Hold each circle over an eye (these are the Birdman's goggles) by inverting your hand so that your fingers extend down the side of your face (your elbows will stick out) and sing:

Up in the air, Junior Birdman,
Up in the air, upside down
Up in the air, Junior Birdman,
With your shoulders to the ground!

☆

D_o attend your child's athletic events, plays, and other activities. Before volunteering to act as team coach or scout leader, check it out with your child to make sure he or she is comfortable with you in such a role. If your time is limited, you can probably share the job with another parent.

Enroll your children and yourself in the YMCA Indian Guide/Princess program (also called Y-Pals and Voyagers) for five- to nine-year-olds. Contact your local YMCA for information. The program has been around for sixty years and offers wonderful activities and the chance to meet other dads and kids.

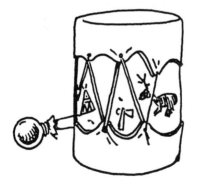

Team up with your child
to do the after-dinner cleanup.
Children too little to reach the
sink can still help clear the table and scrape plates.
Or use a stepladder to put your assistant in a
position to assist! It's a good tradition to start and
a fine time for sharing thoughts.

Do you remember how to blow up your cheeks so that they can be deflated with a finger poke? Inflate one cheek at a time and shift the air to the opposite cheek at each poke. Then inflate both cheeks and blow the air out of your mouth with a poke to both cheeks simultaneously. Let your children do the poking if they are old enough.

☆

Carve your child's initials into wood, such as a tree in your yard or the bench in Grandpa's garden. (Of course, be careful not to deface public property.)

The key is to find a place the child will visit again, so he or she will feel you've made a "mark" together. Teach your child the cardinal rule of carving: Move the knife *away* from the body as you carve.

A fundamental rule about playing games with your children when they are small is simple: YOU LOSE. You should always lose. Little kids won't learn a darn thing about real life when you beat them at a game. It only makes them avoid playing any game with you for several days. So don't win—at least not very often.

There's nothing more memorable for kids than a wrestling match with Dad. Be sure to adapt your strength and speed to the skill level and sensitivity of each child. Children love the opportunity to overpower one of the most powerful figures in their lives.

☆

If you use a home computer, give your child his or her own diskette on which to store files. Save picture or text files on the disk labeled with your child's name.

Have you cuddled your child today?

Both girls and boys need appropriate affection from their father.

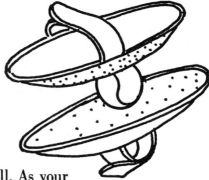

Play catch with your child. When he or she is a toddler, throw or roll a cushiony ball. As your child's abilities grow, increase the distance between you and the speed of the throw. Velcro ball-and-paddle sets are popular because they make it easier to catch the ball and so increase a child's success rate. Buy a catcher's mitt for your son or daughter when he or she becomes interested in Tee Ball or Little League, and break it in together.

☆

Track down your favorite books from childhood. Relate to your child the story of how you came to own them, inscribe them with love from Dad, make a gift of the books to your child, and, of course, read them to your child.

Remember, even an older child who can read still loves being read to by Dad.

☆

If your time together in the evenings is limited—or even if it isn't—have breakfast out weekly or monthly with one child at a time. It's a wonderful one-on-one tradition.

☆

When you can't win, wear them out. Clock your child's running time on a course around the outside of the house or up and down the stairs, for example.

Record his or her time on paper to make it an official event.

Mail a surprise
(such as a card, tape, or book) to
your child from your place of business.
Who doesn't love getting goodies in the mail?
It's very grown-up!

☆

Arrange to have lunch with your child
at day care,
preschool,
or elementary school.

Discuss it with your child beforehand, especially if
he or she is older, or make it a surprise.

☆

If your child is into stamp collecting, be on the lookout at work for any interesting canceled stamps that come on the mail.

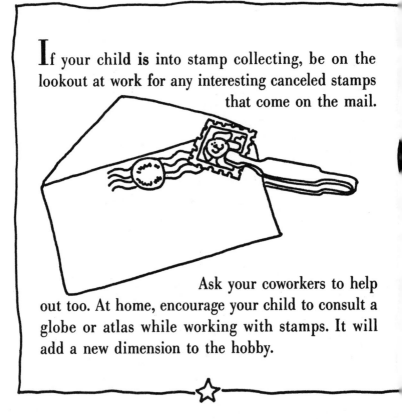

Ask your coworkers to help out too. At home, encourage your child to consult a globe or atlas while working with stamps. It will add a new dimension to the hobby.

☆

If you can,
invest in a basketball
hoop for your child. A little
one-on-one with your son or
daughter can be good for
both your relationship
and your health.

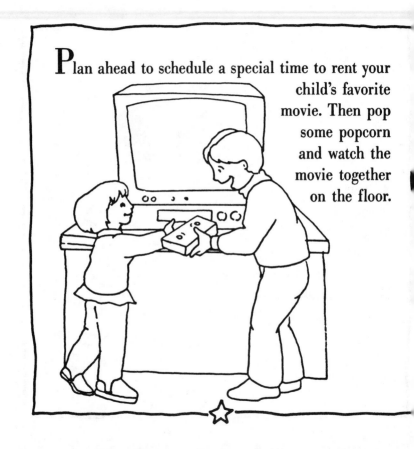

Plan ahead to schedule a special time to rent your child's favorite movie. Then pop some popcorn and watch the movie together on the floor.

Play newspaper
baseball indoors.
It's an excellent
rainy-day activity.

Roll newspaper into a bat, and wad it into a ball.
Hold each together with tape.

Bake a treat (how about cupcakes?) with your child when it's required for class events or parties—or even when it's not!
It doesn't have to be a "Mom job." Pre-measured mixes and frostings make it really easy. Pick special tasks your child can perform, such as beating the batter, setting the timer, and decorating the cake with special designs.

Made by Dad !

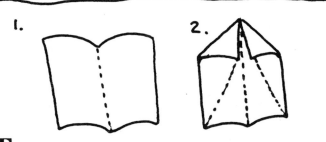

Teach your child to make a paper airplane. You'll never find a child who isn't fascinated by them. Then, if you can, fly your airplane from the TOP of something.

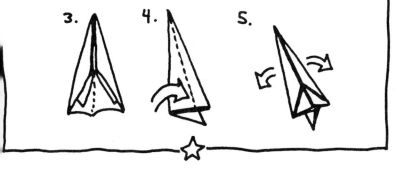

Take your child with you on a business trip when the situation allows and when you know you'll have evenings and maybe even some daytime free. With advance notice, most hotels can help with arrangements for a child of any age.

☆

Dads can help kids learn how to do a lot of important things, such as whistle (sucking in is often easier than blowing out for beginners), snap their fingers, flip a coin, give a high five, tie their shoes (let them practice on your shoes—they are bigger and easier to work on), blow a bubble, row a boat, and carve a pumpkin.

What else can you add to this list?

S̲tart a Bear Hug
or Family Group Hug
tradition.

There's nothing better
than being encircled by the
ones you love (and who love you).

☆

For an afternoon activity, do a photo shoot together. (You can buy your child a camera, borrow
one, or buy a disposable camera.) Shoot anything:
family and friends, pets and potholes, each other.
Make a   scrapbook of the photos.

Helping your child dismantle broken but interesting objects or machines is especially fun when the item to be dismantled is really dirty and greasy—like a bike chain assembly or a lawn mower. Be sure everyone is dressed in ready-to-be-retired clothes.

☆

Go with your child to pick out a "just because" gift for Mom.

It's a nice way to instill the habit of spontaneous gift giving, and your child will enjoy being part of the surprise.

FOR MOM

Now and then, get down on the floor with your child to watch his or her favorite TV program. Have your child explain to you the nuances of the show's character relationships and what he or she likes best about the show.

A simple birdhouse is a good woodworking project.

A basic birdhouse will appeal to both boys and girls, will need only minimal sanding, can be done in a few hours, and usually is ready to be put up immediately. Check your library for how-to books with diagrams. Be sure to pick a birdhouse size and style that suits the birds in your area. Then buy an identification book and note in it when your child spots various birds.

☆

If your parent(s) live nearby, visit them with your children. It can be a good time to talk about your own childhood with your kids.

Also, parents seldom get to see you, Dad, without your spouse.

☆

Thumb wrestle with your child.
Kids love it!

☆

Supervise your child in using more advanced machines than he or she is normally allowed to use, such as a sander. This will make your son or daughter feel capable, competent, and self-sufficient. Your child will not get these feelings of self-worth through watching TV.

Play your little one like a musical instrument. Pretend toes are your harmonica. Blow into your child's belly button to create sound effects. Clap feet together like a percussion instrument to keep the beat to fast music. Be the party guilty of teaching your child to blow "raspberries."

☆

If your son or daughter is interested in boats, trains, or airplanes, work together to build a model  of one, static or even radio-controlled. Kits are available at different ability levels. Your goal is to continually evaluate your kids' skill level and let them do all the work they are capable of. This way, they will not get bored while you "help" or be frustrated by models that are too advanced for them.

☆

Teach your child to ride a bike or roller-blade; it's an opportunity you really shouldn't miss. You might need to work out in preparation for this activity. You'll need to be in shape because teaching a child to ride a two-wheeler or skate in roller blades requires a lot of running alongside by you.

☆

Videotape your child's sports practice or game and view it later with one or more of your child's friends. Make it a social event. Remember, they can see their faults; you don't have to point them out.

Building a tree house falls in the category of a classic "Dad do." A skilled dad can get quite fancy, but a tree house can be simple: Find two large trees growing about three feet apart. Nail two two- by four-inch boards between the trees, on the outside of the trunks for supports. Nail two- by six-inch floorboards across the supports. Add a small ladder and railing and you'll be remembered forever.

Include your child in the toasting and clinking
of glasses (or training cups) for family
celebrations, such as anniversaries,
birthdays, career advances,
and other happy
occasions.

☆

Your child (girl or boy) can "shave" with you in the mornings while standing on a footstool or closed toilet. Cut a mock razor from a discarded plastic credit card and apply some of your shaving cream to your child's face. If you use an electric razor, fashion a mock razor for your child from any small wooden block.

☆

Dads seem to be more likely than moms to practice the art of tickling. It's fun, and also a good technique when there is a need for diverting a kid's attention. Be sensitive; hard tickling is not always enjoyed. Stop or soften your actions if your child requests it.

"It's a bird! . . .
It's a plane! . . .
It's Super [child's name]!"

This is a gymnastic game played with Dad on the floor and the child overhead, supported by Dad's knees and arms as the child "flies."

☆

Team up with another
dad and his child
for an outing like
a Sunday brunch,
a religious activity,
a trip to a petting
zoo, or a
sports event.

P.S. Why not include one or two grandfathers while
you're at it?

Write a family newsletter with your children to send out to friends and relatives. Your kids can be editors, illustrators, reporters, stamp lickers, or designers depending on their ages and talent. If you have a home computer, even young children can use it to illustrate and design your newsletter.

FAMILY GAZETTE

CAMILLE RIDES 2-WHEELER

ROXANNE GETS AN A+!
in an amazing

Whether you live in the country or the city, you can enjoy stargazing with your child. Purchase or borrow from the library a book on constellations. Or, invest in a small telescope so you can enjoy a view of the moon's craters, too. This will give you a chance to discuss our place in the universe with your son or daughter.

Select a puzzle your child will
delight in, or let him or her
choose one you can work
on together.

Then, if you find that you have created a "puzzle
monster," invest in a tray or board that allows you
to move your puzzle from place to place as you
work on it so you don't monopolize the dining room
table.

☆

If you live in an area where fireflies are found, take a clear glass or plastic widemouthed container with a vented top and go out together into the summer night to catch these critters. Let your child release them after you've finished enjoying the illuminations or at bedtime, whichever comes first.

☆

Take advantage of any local carnivals, art fairs, county fairs, and free concerts that come your way. Remember that an hour or two is as long as you can reasonably expect your child's attention span to last, and plan accordingly.

Share a creative drawing game. Have a child write a large capital or lowercase letter on a blank piece of paper. Then use it as the basis for a drawing of anything that comes to mind. With an older child, take turns deciding on letters and creating something for each other.

Encourage in your child a love of the wintertime outdoors.

Nature hikes should not be just for spring and summer. Winter can be a good time to explore and look for animal tracks in the snow while enjoying the lack of bugs and ticks in the woods. Build a snowman or, better yet, a snow fort!

☆

When paying at a restaurant, gas station, or ticket booth, let your child become part of the transaction. Provide the cash for the act of payment. Have your child collect the change for you too. As your child's math comprehension increases, add counting change to your child's responsibilities. "Paying the bills" is an empowering act.

☆

Join your child in cleaning up a messy room or garage. It's nice to have a helpmate when doing a less-than-favorite job. It also shows friendship.

☆

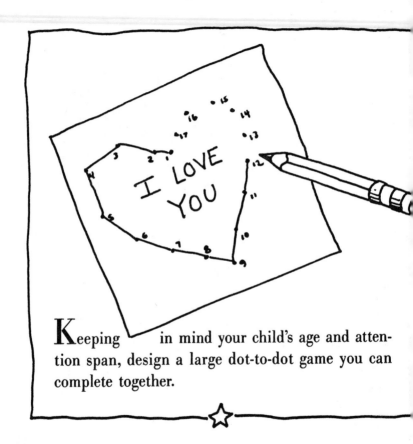

I LOVE YOU

Keeping in mind your child's age and attention span, design a large dot-to-dot game you can complete together.

Go to an enrichment or exercise class together. There are often art and cooking classes offered at community centers. Karate can be a good choice. Some beginning classes have very few restrictions on age or gender.

Help your child set up a lemonade stand at least once during his or her childhood. Be sure to record the event in photos or on video.

Ask your child to create a piece of art for you to frame and hang up at your place of work.

Consider learning to play (or at least to understand) your child's current favorite pastime, whether it is playing video games, dressing up dolls, collecting rocks or beer cans, or reading about dinosaurs.

Children, just as adults, like to share the things they enjoy with the ones they love.

Read
to your children.

Try to set aside at least a
little time each day to read together. Designate a
special place to read, which can be as simple as a
stack of pillows in the living room. Don't continue
to read anything that you or your children are not
enjoying. Read to your children even after they
learn to read themselves. Be sure you've spent equal
reading time with sons and daughters.

⭐

Use the following pages to jot down ideas for special ways to spend time with your offspring. (Maybe you have memories of things your own father did with you that made him special in your eyes.)

Things to do

Things to do

Vicki Lansky has written more than twenty-five books in which she shares what has worked for her and others. For a free catalog of her other books, just drop a note to the address below or call 1-800-255-3379.

Vicki Lansky
c/o Practical Parenting™
Department D
Deephaven, MN 55391

101 Ways
to Be a Special Dad

If you enjoyed *101 Ways to Be a Special Dad*, you'll also appreciate Vicki Lansky's other Contemporary classics, *101 Ways to Tell Your Child "I Love You"* and *101 Ways to Make Your Child Feel Special*. They are available in your local bookstore or by mail. To order directly with your credit card, please call Contemporary Books at (312) 782-9181.